A Beginner' Growing Fr

Gardening Tips and Methods for Growing Fruit Trees For Pleasure and Profit

Healthy Gardening Series

Dueep Jyot Singh

Mendon Cottage Books

JD-Biz Publishing

Download Free Books!

http://MendonCottageBooks.com

All Rights Reserved.

No part of this publication may be reproduced in any form or by any means, including scanning, photocopying, or otherwise without prior written permission from JD-Biz Corp Copyright © 2015

All Images Licensed by Fotolia and 123RF.

Disclaimer

The information is this book is provided for informational purposes only. It is not intended to be used and medical advice or a substitute for proper medical treatment by a qualified health care provider. The information is believed to be accurate as presented based on research by the author.

The contents have not been evaluated by the U.S. Food and Drug Administration or any other Government or Health Organization and the contents in this book are not to be used to treat cure or prevent disease.

The author or publisher is not responsible for the use or safety of any diet, procedure or treatment mentioned in this book. The author or publisher is not responsible for errors or omissions that may exist.

Warning

The Book is for informational purposes only and before taking on any diet, treatment or medical procedure, it is recommended to consult with your primary health care provider.

Check out some of the other Health Learning Series books at Amazon.com

[Gardening Series on Amazon](#)

[Health Learning Series on Amazon](#)

Download Free Books!

http://MendonCottageBooks.com

Table of Contents

Introduction 5
Which Fruit to Grow? 9
Fruit Production Charts 11
Cold Hardiness zones 12
Apples 13
Citrus fruits 14
Strawberries 16
    Planting Your Strawberries 17
    Mulching Strawberries. 17
    Propagation 18
    Feeding Strawberries 18
    Protecting Your Strawberries. 18
    Growing Strawberries in Barrels 18

Buying the Right Trees and Bushes 20
Soil Conditions 21
Nitrogen Fixing Crops 24
Planning your garden 25
Natural Weedkillers 26
General Planting 27
Supporting Your Fruit Trees 28
Bird Protection 29
Frost Protection 30
Planting Fruit Trees Against Walls 31
What Are Espaliers? 33
Keeping Your Bushes and Trees Healthy 35
Fertilizers and pesticides – 37
    Cow Manure – the Best Organic Fertilizer/Compost Base 37
    John Innes Compost 38
    Basic Healthy Compost Mixtures 39

How to Make Leaf Compost 40

Natural Pesticides 42
    Neem Pesticide 42

    Preparing Neem seeds 43

Chilis 45
Tobacco 46
Bougainvillea Leaves 47
Fungicides for Soil 48
    Onion – Garlic Antifungal Solution 48

    Papaya Cure – 49

    Using Cow Manure Ash as a Pesticide 49

Nutrient Deficiency Symptoms in Plants 51
Spraying 52
Garden Pests 54
Pollination 56
Fruit Plant Propagation 58
Harvesting your fruit 60
Appendix – 62
Conclusion 63
Author Bio 64
Publisher 74

Introduction

When Mother Nature blessed the new born earth with life forms milleniums ago, the diversity of one celled creatures took up different lines of evolution due to climatic changes and mutations. That is when plant life evolved along with animal life. And that is how the surface of the earth was covered with lush fruitful vegetation, which flourished and evolved in different climates.

As time went by, climatic changes also changed the nature and the appearance of these plants. From multicelled algae and fungi, they became huge multicelled giant trees, like the Sequoia, which are remnants of those glorious days of giant Green trees gone by.

And soon man found out that trees were very useful to give him shelter, to give him food, and to provide him with essential fruit, leaves, and seeds to supplement his diet. That was because he was imitating the animals around him.

They nibbled at leaves, he did the same thing. Sometimes he ended up with a tummy ache. Sometimes the animals ended up sick while he was left hale and hearty. But down the ages, and through lots of trial and error, he found out that every single plant out there could be put into use, even those plants we consider weeds today.

The mythological and historical hanging Gardens of Babylon, which were supposed to have been built by Nebuchadnezzar, but in actuality were built by Sennacherib in Nineveh, Assyria, about 300 km away from Babylon.

These were lush with green trees from all over the world. And historians who are not really bothered about historic authenticity and the names of kings, did not bother much about the locality or the creator of one of the seven wonders of the ancient world.

First-hand accounts of that time were not available, and when Babylon conquered Assyria, they called it the new Babylon. And so centuries later historians wrote about the wonders of marvelous trees and green vegetation, growing in Babylon.

So that is the reason why since ancient times, trees, especially fruit trees have been an important part of cultured and civilized landscaping. They were and are planted in gardens for the pleasure of the general public or for your own private enjoyment.

You can grow one kind of fruit or another in almost any garden. Even the smallest garden can produce apples and strawberries. If you have plenty of land you are lucky because you have the space to allow your trees to spread their wings and flourish.

Besides being planted for their crops, fruit trees and fruit shrubs can be used to make your garden look more attractive, aesthetically pleasing and a thing of beauty and a joy forever.

You can make hedges from black currant bushes. Logan berries and blackberries can be used for covering fences and garden sheds. Bare walls can be covered with fruit trees instead of creepers or wall plants.

Garnering a harvest from strawberry plants

Blackcurrant bush

Which Fruit to Grow?

Unless you have plenty of land, there is a chance that you are going to be strapped for space. That is why you need to know which fruit to grow. The time for huge gardens is passed, unless you have inherited lots of land. That is why your small gardens need to be filled up with useful fruit trees. So of course the best option is to grow the fruit you love best. Also, choose the fruit, of which the freshness appeals most to you.

Ease of growing is an important factor. What are the growing conditions necessary to give you a good harvest? Some fruit like peaches grow well in sunny and hot atmospheres. If your garden is full of shade, look for fruit, which grow well in the shade.

Choose your choice of fruits that grow well in the shade –

http://lawrencefruittreeproject.wordpress.com/recommended-fruit-plants/shade-tolerant-fruit-plants/

Fruit can also be grown profitably in containers, when you have limited space. Gardeners have been training fruit into cordons, espaliers fans and up fences and down walls.

Choose trees which have been grafted to semi-dwarf rootstocks or dwarf rootstocks to make sure that you do not have giant size plants, when you wanted something of reasonable size and easily manageable.

Fruit Production Charts

Fruit production charts are going to depend a lot on your locality.

You can download these production charts on these URLs, and their planting seasons.

For people in the UK –

http://www.rhs.org.uk/Gardening/Grow-Your-Own/Advice/Fruit-advice/Planning

For gardeners in the USA

http://www.bhg.com/gardening/plant-dictionary/fruit/

I would suggest Apple, cherries, as well as semitropical citrus fruit, depending on the weather. However, fruit gardening is not done by somebody who is not dedicated because you cannot just plant fruits and walk away, hoping that they are going to grow on their own self.

You will need pruning them, monitoring them for pests and taking the advice of your friendly neighborhood professional horticulturists for the best way to keep them healthy and safe.

Choose the fruit plant varieties, which are recommended to you by your local plant agricultural extension service in your city or in your state. That is because some varieties need so many hours of sun and others need so many hours of chill.

The self-fertile varieties are going to grow fruit better if they are grown near any other flower or plant, which is a matching pollinator. This is going to be explained when you read further on with an example of mustard plants and apples. Nursery catalogs and extension publications can give you tables of varieties of fruit and plants which are compatible with each other and should be grown together.

Cold Hardiness zones

Can your fruit trees survive the winter? This extensive knowledge is going to be given to you on this URL, depending where you are located on the globe.

http://en.wikipedia.org/wiki/Hardiness_zone

Apples

Liberty and *Freedom* apple varieties can be grown in 6.5 pH variety soil, but you can also grow them in soil, which is more acidic as long as it is well-drained and fertile.

Mild winter climates in the USA can produce pink Lady and Anna, which are no chill apple varieties.

Late-season and midseason apples are good choices for storing and taste, when compared to early-season plant varieties.

Citrus fruits

These plants are extremely to grow in sunny zones – [8B – 10], especially hybrids, which include mandarin oranges, Meyer lemon and even kumquat. They do not enjoy the cold. But if you have planted them from seed or from seedlings, your little plant has grown throughout the year and now you are worried about the frost, just cover them with blankets. This is when the temperature has dropped to below 0°C. With a little bit of care, you are going to get a winter lemon harvest.

Cherries – cherries are a good choice for the 4– 7 zone. They need lots of air, soil which is near neutral and richly fertilized. If you do not have plenty of space in your garden, grow the dwarf variety of plants which are going to give you fruit ranging from yellow in color to black. *"Stella"* is sweet and *"North Star"* and *"Montmorency"* have a sour taste and are best for pies.

Remember to protect your cherry trees from birds, because they are going to be your partners in harvesting the crop. I found a gardener friend sprinkling kaolin clay over the cherries because he did not have protective netting at hand. You may want to try that.

Prunus avium is the sweet cherry variety. *P. cerasus* is the sour variety.

Strawberries

Strawberries grow naturally at the edge of wood lands, and therefore they thrive on lots of organic matter and leaf mold. They like light soil and good drainage.

Strawberries are surface rooting. That is why the cultivation should be shallow. So before planting strawberries in late summer, add 2 good buckets full of leaf mold, organic dung, well rotted compost, and even spent hops if available to per square yard of your strawberry patch.

Planting Your Strawberries

After you have bought healthy young plants which should be virus free and have been grown in soil rich in organic matter, make a good hole with a trowel. Spread the roots of individual plants carefully, put back the soil and tread down hard. Hoe lightly over to remove signs of gardening boots!

The rows should be 2 ½ feet apart, and the plants one and a half feet apart in the rows. In Europe, strawberries give a heavier yield when planted in August. That depends on the weather. And you get a harvest not only in the first year, but for three years afterwards.

If the weather is mild, planting can be done even before the onset of winter. But this does not give time for the plants to establish themselves and you are going to have winter harvest losses. Spring planting is possible, though not crop can be taken in the first summer under such circumstances.

Mulching Strawberries.

When the strawberries start to flower, it is time for mulching. Use clean straw, peat, and even peat Moss to provide extra support and nutrients to your plants by applying around them to keep the trusses of fruit clean off the soil. A friend uses strips of polythene to do that.

Do not reply the mulch too early otherwise you may face the risk of damage by frost.

At the end of the season, you can scrape up the straw and put it in the compost heap. I have heard that burning it at the end of the season – where the straw lies and which has been raked into ridges – is not going to harm the plant and will also help in getting rid of pests. But I do not like burning anything.

When you are putting it in the compost heap, you can also add fish manure – 3 ounces per square yard.

Propagation

The moment you get good runners, peg the little plants down into the soil or into 3 inch pots sunk into the soil using strong wires bent like hairpins. This will enable the roots to form more quickly.

Plant out the newly rooted plants in freshly prepared beds. If they have been rooted directly in the pots, they can be potted on at the end of summer when the weather grows mild.

Feeding Strawberries

Fish fertilizer is excellent for your strawberries. It should have 10%, potash at 3 ounce per square yard. Immediately after fruiting give your plants organic manure, hoof and horn meal at 3 ounces per square yard.

Protecting Your Strawberries.

If you are expecting a frost, cover your plants with newspaper. Winds do not normally blow on frosty nights, and so your papers are not going to blow away. Of course, early in the season you would want to cover them with a fish netting to protect your plants from birds.

Growing Strawberries in Barrels

Try growing strawberries in 4 ½ feet high barrels with a diameter of 3 feet.

Make four or five drainage holes about 1 ½ inches wide in the base of the barrel. Cover each hole with broken pieces of pots. Then make 20 – 25 holes about 3 inches wide here and there in the sides of the buyer. These are the goals through which your plants are going to grow. Fill the barrel up with a good potting compost gradually as your proceeding with the planting work. John Innes putting compost number two is excellent here.

Here is a good way which you can make John Innes potting compost, at home, instead of buying it, and if you are not making your own individual compost formula.

http://www.backyardgardener.com/soil/soil2.html

As far as I know, it is not commercially available in the United States. Yet.

Push the plants through the holes in the barrel from the outside firm the soil over the roots. Fill with compost and continue planting through all the holes. Plant six more plants on the top surface. Stand the barrel on bricks to ensure good drainage and put it in a shady place.

Water immediately after planting to help the soil to settle and water regularly throughout the season.

Buying the Right Trees and Bushes

Naturally, you are going to get the right disease-free trees and bushes from a reputed nursery. When buying bushes and trees it is important to deal with reliable sources of plants. The experienced gardener and horticulturalist should propagate the fruit trees and bushes his own self.

There are many different types of serious virus diseases that affect soft fruit. Therefore, look for licensed growers who are approved by the Ministry of agriculture or by your government to provide you with fruit plants in your state, or in your country.

I found this URL very useful for buying plants from approved nurseries in the USA and Canada.

http://www.inspection.gc.ca/plants/plant-protection/directives/horticulture/d-01-04/appendix-6/eng/134564255

Native plant nurseries can be found on this URL –

http://www.plantnative.org/national_nursery_dir_main.htm

In the case of plums, pears, apples and cherries, buy young bushes and trees. That is because they will establish themselves in the garden faster than older trees.

Plants that have been kept in the nursery for a number of years are apt to be stunted because of lack of room to develop and they may never recover properly.

Soil Conditions

The right soil condition is going to depend on the area in which you plant your trees. William Saroyan had an uncle who decided to grow pomegranates in the desert, and got a nursery to supply him 100 pomegranate seedlings. A large percentage of them died, and their harvest for their dreams was two small pomegranates of which both the keen gardeners ate one apiece.

So look at the area and the right soil conditions. Earthworms which are going to be your best friends should be able to penetrate in the soil up to a depth of 6 feet or more. They should be encouraged in your garden as they help to ventilate and drain the soil.

You can get your earthworms from your nursery. You may find this enterprising farmer's story interesting, when he decided to build an earthworm Farm.

In the East, earthworms are normally cultivated by putting a mixture of cow dung and kitchen waste in a pot. Then, children are asked to dig up the earthworms from the garden, after the soil has been watered well. Or people just wait for the rainy season, when the earthworms are going to be found on the surface. They had been collected and then put in the organic fertilizer and allowed to flourish in a moist and rich banquet.

And so you have your wormy compost within a year or so, especially if you are making this compost in huge bins.

My mother used the poultry waste, and ordinary manure along with greenery from the kitchen gardens, and leaves in the autumn. All of them were put in a huge bin. And because we lived in an area where it rained 300 days out of 365, there was no dearth of earthworms.

Every morning we children used to go collecting them, from the porch outside where they had been washed up from the garden during the night, thanks to the torrents filling their holes during the dark and stormy hours. And that is when I learned about our best friends, the earthworms.

No wonder they were such excellent bait for when we went fishing. Another excellent bait was wasp grubs , but that is another story.

Constant application of organic matter will encourage earthworm growth and the worms in turn will carry any organic plant foods applied as a surface dressing the down into the soil.

Squeamishness was not an option here or being girlishly particular. Once you pick up an earthworm and know that it is going to help you, you are going to get used to it. And some of them were really fat and juicy.

Frequent deep cultivation reduces the earthworm population and does not improve the structure of the soil. So if your soil is 6 – 12 inches deep, before it reaches a more solid surface, you will need to add more layers of soil, compost, humus and other natural ingredients to the soil to make it more nutritional.

Peat, seaweed, limestone and natural plant waste have been used for centuries to make the soil more nutritional. Naturally, soil, which is rich in nitrogen, is going to be more fertile.

Nitrogen Fixing Crops

At our agricultural college, our instructors always told us the benefit about alternating crops with one crop of nitrogen fixing plants like legumes, soy beans and alfalfa. One season of these plants meant the soil got enough of nitrogen to give you a good season's harvest of grain, vegetables and fruit. So if that can be done in the farms, why not do it in your own garden.

There is very useful information on nitrogen fixing plants on this URL

http://en.wikipedia.org/wiki/Category:Nitrogen-fixing_crops.

Plant any plants of this list given above in your garden for a season. After you have harvested the crop, plant your fruit trees in that particular nitrogen enriched soil.

Planning your garden

Plant the fruit bushes or fruit trees in soil that has been cleared of weeds. It is said that one weed left in your garden is going to give you seven years of weeds. So clear the ground, either by working on it. The whole summer, carefully forking out the weeds or allowing the weeds to grow in the spring and then applying a strong natural weed killer.

Natural Weedkillers

As I advocate natural fertilizers and natural weedkillers, here is plenty of information on natural weed killers.

http://www.goodhousekeeping.com/home/gardening/homemade-weed-killers

http://fullofgreatideas.blogspot.in/2011/07/natural-weed-killer-made-with-basic.html

https://www.pinterest.com/judydinsmore/weed-control-natural/

I was very glad to see that people are using natural homemade weedkillers instead of hormone weed killers recommended to them from professionals in the nursery, more often nowadays.

I knew about salt and vinegar, before, but I never got a chance to use it. Remember that salt should used in small quantities. In olden days, warriors who wanted to conquer an area and destroy it completely used to sprinkle fistfuls of salt on the farmland. This dried the soil out completely, and nothing grew there ever again.

Even today in the East, if somebody is really bitter about something, they say, "I shall burn that place to the ground, and sow salt there." That means that nothing can live there forevermore.

General Planting

If you are living in an area which is not prey to a harsh and cold winter, you can plant bushes and trees anywhere between October to March, but the best time to plant them is early November, if possible, so that they can settle down and grow roots before the hard winter sets in.

This is going to give them at least three months before springtime brings in new growth and rejuvenation of plant tissue.

Supporting Your Fruit Trees

Adequate staking is important because if a tree moves even slightly in the wind, its minute root hairs will be torn away and killed. This is when you are planting a seedling for the first time and it is still trying to get its grip on the soil. Also, depressions are going to be caused in the soil, which form around the base of the trunk. Water is going to collect there, and cause root rot.

Even though these grape vines are not what you can call a fruit "tree," proper staking make sure that each plant has good support.

Bird Protection

Soft fruit, particularly strawberries, grapes, raspberries and currants can be protected from birds with a wire netting cage. This cage should be 6 feet high, and as long and wide as is necessary with a gate at one end. To keep the birds out, the netting should not be more than ¾ inches mesh. I normally use fish netting because it is cheaper than wire netting. This can be used for the top of the cage. Wire netting can be used for the sides and surrounding area.

This fish netting is removed each winter and dried before storing away. Nylon netting can also be used for the entire case, but I found that pigeons have this bad habit of pecking away at nylon and getting in through the holes. I have not found any nylon netting supplier which can give me a big-bird- proof Bird protection netting!

Frost Protection

If you are in an area subject to frost, make sure that the fruit should be planted in higher parts and not in a frost pocket. You can remove part of the fence or the base of the hedge on the lowest boundary so that frozen air can drain away.

Fruit bushes and other soft fruits may be covered with dry sacking, polythene, jute sacks and newspaper on nights when Frost is expected. This is going to reduce the losses of heat by soil radiation and will also protect the blossoms from the cold.

I remember seeing a movie about a decade ago, in which the characters were trying to preserve their vineyard from Frost. Stoves were lit in the yard, and all the people in the village kept fanning the delicate vines with pieces of cloth, so that the heat could protect the grapes. They did this throughout the night.

I am definitely not so dedicated, because my life and livelihood does not depend upon a good crop of grapes this year. So if you are my sort, and would rather like a good night's rest out of the cold, do not plant any fruit trees which shrivel away in the frost. Or rather, plant those plants, which can be covered easily with jute sacks and polythene and then you can stop worrying.

Planting Fruit Trees Against Walls

I heard about my grandfather telling my grandmother not to plant any tree against our boundary walls. Grandma, being naturally contrary, immediately did exactly that. Also, walls absorb moisture and so the soil at the base of a wall is often dry. So fruit trees are not going to flourish here.

But grandma's Neem tree grew enormously and she told everybody that grandpa had planted it for pure and fresh air in our house – but one fine day, it was going to break the wall. So there.

This was her way of paving the path of complaining, when 30 years later, those roots had broken through the wall, and invaded our garden and home , both inside and outside.

But if you really have to plant trees against a wall, bury a 3 inch agricultural drainpipe upright and 1 foot away from the wall and the site of your tree. Pour in water from time to time during the soil to moisten the soil layer below.

In addition, mulch the surface of the ground with leaf mold, rotted compost, and peat.

You can get more information on mulching on this site-

http://apps.rhs.org.uk/advicesearch/profile.aspx?pid=323

Prepare the border by deep digging and incorporate some compost or well-rotted organic fertilizer. Plant the tree so that its base is about 8 inches away from the wall. Spread out the root fan- wise from the wall. Support the plant with a cane or if there are horizontal wires on the wall, fasten it to them. Water it well.

Remember to water your garden well after mulching.

Cherries, especially Morello cherries grown in fan shaped trees and planted 12 feet apart or gooseberries/currants are excellent cordons and windbreakers to protect other plants in your garden.

Sunny walls can benefit peaches, nectarines, streets, cherries, figs and apricots. These are planted 12 feet apart. Grow them in fan shaped trees. You can also plant highest-quality pears 10 feet apart and train them as espaliers.

What Are Espaliers?

Since ancient times, gardeners enjoyed the practice of training branches of fruit trees, or even ornamental shrubs to grow against walls, and flat. These branches were supported on lattices and added that touch of distinct class to your garden walls.

Walls which have plenty of shade can be covered with pears. Some popular varieties are *Mary Louise* and *Conference*. You may also want to plant plums here like *Golden Gage* and *Victoria*. Gooseberries, red cherries, and currants are also good choices.

On walls where you can get sun and shade, you can plant apricots, peaches, dessert cherries, pears and apples.

Keeping Your Bushes and Trees Healthy

Fertilizers and manures are needed to keep your plants healthy. Some plants may need extra nitrogen and others may need potassium in larger quantities. There is no hard and fast rule about this since a very wet season may well produce high nitrogen conditions automatically or a dry sunny season may produce high potash conditions. It depends on your locality, and how fertile the soil is.

http://en.wikipedia.org/wiki/Fertilizer#Organic_fertilizer

This URL gives you a lot of good information on organic fertilizer.

In the coastal parts of the Indian subcontinent, I noticed large amounts of dried fish just placed there in the sun, and serving no useful purpose at all. When I asked the fishermen, they said that that was the dried fish which they would not sell, and they did not know what to do with it. It just stayed there until the powder was blown away in the air, and in the meantime, it stank the surroundings.

I asked them if I could borrow some, because I needed that dried fish for my garden. They immediately told me that they would sell it to me at about an equivalent of a dollar a pound! Well, I was foolish, by allowing them to know that fish meal and dried fish is the best organic fertilizer available today to make compost.

Anyway, the good part is that the audience listening to our wrangle immediately began asking me about how I used fish meal and dried fish for natural fertilizer. And I told them – just put it in the bin, in the corner of your garden, remember to moisten regularly with the little bit of water, keep adding organic waste from your kitchen like that stalks, leaves, roots, herbs, or anything else which you would normally throw out in the garbage, do not bother about the stink, and you are going to get the best organic fertilizer and compost, available at really affordable rates.

Fertilizers and pesticides –

Cow Manure – the Best Organic Fertilizer/Compost Base

Make a hole in the ground. If you are living in flats, you are going to make this fertilizer in a hole free metal barrel. Fill half of it with farm manure like cow dung. Then add some more natural organic materials to this mixture, because we are making compost.

These natural organic materials can include dried leaves, kitchen organic waste, and anything else. Add some earthworms, requested from the nearest nursery to this mixture. Now add some water to this mixture, and cover. Leave the sun and nature to do its magic.

I know about a rooftop gardener who requested all the people in her block of flats to put all their kitchen waste into that metal compost bin, instead of throwing it into the recycler. Many of the apartment members could not care less. So she did this compost making on her own self.

However, when her particular block got the best rooftop garden prize in the colony, every single apartment member decided that, hey, this natural compost was a good idea, because the chrysanthemums, geraniums and other plants bloomed and grew so gloriously and Mrs. S. had such a good idea.

So now, every evening all the kitchen pails with organic matter are emptied out in that perpetually bubbling compost bin.

John Innes Compost

If you were an herbalist, gardener, or agriculturalist 2000 years ago and were asked to plant plants in your garden, you would immediately break the soil sow the seeds and leave everything else to nature. Thankfully, man began to know all about proper growing of plants and traditional agricultural methods with fertilizer, water, sun, and air, began to be noted, followed and implemented down the generations.

Even so, after the 20th century, the real and proper combination of essential nutrients necessary for proper plant growth was largely a matter of trial and error.

However, in the early 20th century, two research workers in John Innes Horticultural Institute in London decided to concentrate on combinations of soil content, which could prevent parasite attacks, encourage plant growth and help in an increased yield of produce. It took six years for them to get the right proportions together for the best plant growth rates and yield.

Thanks to their painstaking work, this compost is available all over the world, but if you want, you can make it right at home.

The main popular standard composts available in the market till date are potting composts and seed sowing composts.

The basic formula for both of them is the same. It is only the proportions which are different.

Basic Healthy Compost Mixtures

The Basic formula ingredients are –

Organic fertilizers, coarse grit and sand, moss peat/Spagnum and topsoil or loam , depending on the plant variety.

Enthusiastic gardeners are going to find this URL very useful –

http://gardenofeaden.blogspot.in/2011/03/how-to-make-john-innes-compost.html

Now, if anybody asked me whether I use this potting compost or this seed sowing compost in my garden, the answer is ummm well no, not really. But that is because I am using traditional gardening methods to make my garden grow.

The soil is rich, well fertilized with farm manure and leaf compost , and with sand, grit, gravel and pieces of brick and small stones. The pesticides I use are 50 mL of Neem oil to 1 gallon of water is sprayed all over the plants and leaves when they start to grow. I also keep shoving in kitchen produce on my compost heap, so that it can decompose and add its mineral content to the natural goodness of organic fertilizer.

Also, I encourage insects and worms to grow in that half moist compost heap. That part of my garden stinks to high Eden. But the yield of organically grown vegetables, fruit and herbs in my garden are significantly higher than those obtained in gardens treated with chemical fertilizer, nutrients and pesticides.

How to Make Leaf Compost

Next autumn, when you start to groan about having to rake in leaves, try thinking about natural leaf compost.

In many parts of the East, gardeners find it so easy to make huge piles of leaves, and set fire to them. My gardeners are definitely disgusted with me. That is because I ask them to dig deep holes and put the leaves in there in order to make leaf compost. They would rather set a match like their ancestors did.

You may want to know more about how to make leaf compost. I found this URL very helpful.

http://oldworldgardenfarms.com/2012/10/02/composting-leaves-4-simple-tips-to-making-great-compost-with-leaves/

Seriously speaking, I never bothered much about the "acidic" content of leaves, while raking them up in autumn. It was just getting under any tree and collecting the fallen leaves. Then place all of them in a wheelbarrow and back to your leaf compost corner you go, whistling while you work.

So the leaf mixture is always rather eclectic, and I have not seen my plants coming to any visible harm because of the nature of the compost!

Natural Pesticides

Do you believe it, that farmers are using Coke and Pepsi, to get rid of pests in India? That is because we know that they are so powerful that they are going to kill all the insects. And why is this so, you may ask? Because these soft drinks have been contaminated with a very high quantity and percentage of pesticides.

One wonders whether this contamination is due to the liquids and ingredients used in the manufacture of these very popular soft drinks, or has it been done by jealous competitors. Nevertheless, farmers have decided not to ingest coke and Pepsi, but allow their plants to do that and let somebody else ruin his health. Naturally, these pesticides are harmful, so I do not suggest that you empty out your Diet Coke can all over your plants. Rather, I am going to give you some natural pesticides, which you would want to use right now.

Natural pesticides are going to take longer to show an effect than chemical pesticides, but you know that you are not going to be poisoned through toxins.

Neem Pesticide

The Margosa- Neem has been used for centuries, as a natural pesticide in the Indian subcontinent.

Whenever you are preparing a natural pesticide, dry it in the shade. Drying it under direct heat of the sun is going to reduce its potential power. If you are using a liquid, add a little bit of soap, so that the pesticides can adhere to the surfaces on which they have been applied.

Some of these pesticides need to be diluted, so that they do not burn the soft tissue of young plants.

Since ancient times, Neem seeds have been used as a pesticide, as well as an organic fertilizer. Put 250 g of Neem oil, in 1 gallon of water and spray your fruit trees.

800 g of Neem extract/oil from the seeds, can preserve hundred kilograms of stored grain from fungus and other pests. You can also sprinkle plenty of dried Neem leaves in your storage barn and on the storage sacks, and prevent pest attacks.

Preparing Neem seeds

Collect the mature seeds of the Neem, – they are going to be yellow in color – wash, husk – we need the pulp – and allow to dry completely in the shade. 500 g of Neem seeds are best for 10 L of water. Grind the seeds to a powder, add to the water and allow to soak overnight. Strain the liquid with a muslin cloth, and spray all the leaves with this natural pesticide. This is known to kill about hundred varieties of plant pests.

The Neem plant has been a provider for organic pesticides, and fungicides for millenniums.

Chilis

Believe it or not, chilis are one of the best ways in which you can get rid of all the insect pests. Just take two handfuls of red chili fruit and dry them in the shade. Now grind them up with a little bit of water, and added this paste to 2 L of water. Soak overnight. Wonderfully effective. Remember to cover your nose, when you are powdering and grinding these peppers, because they are powerful irritants to sensitive noses.

Tobacco

This natural pesticide was used in the Southern States to get rid of cotton pests, before the Civil War so how come Americans are still not using it? Why are they using chemical pesticides?

Anyway , this recipe is thanks to my pen pal buddy, Billy Jo in Georgia. Just collect fresh and healthy leaves of a tobacco plant. This tobacco is going to contain nicotine, which is your best insecticide. Wash and dry the leaves and stems. Allow 80 g of leaves and stems, to 1 L of water. Allow to soak for two days. This has to be applied early in the morning, because the nicotine is volatile. It is going to escape as a gas, so be very careful because this gas is toxic.

Do not allow it to touch your skin.

Bougainvillea Leaves

Not only are Bougainvilleas extremely ornamental in your garden, but their leaves are powerful pesticides.

Some virus diseases of plants and flowers can be healed, by grinding 200 g of fresh Bougainvillea leaves and adding this leaf paste to a liter of water. Spray. This also keeps your beans and tomatoes free of viruses.

Fungicides for Soil

Fungii are definitely going to flourish in shade or in highly humid atmospheres. So get rid of these two factors, and reduce fungal growth.

Fungicides are normally applied to the bottom portion of the leaves, or added to the soil.

Onion – Garlic Antifungal Solution

Garlic is an extremely powerful natural fungicide

Believe this or not, I learned this, just by chance. I mixed 500 g of onion and garlic in 10 L of water, and allowed to ferment, because of some crazy notion that, just like pickles ripened in the sun, this would also be very effective. And it is true! Seven days of ripening and then diluting this solution again with water – another 10 L – so that it was not so concentrated, I found the most powerful fungicidal ever. Try it out right now.

Papaya Cure –

You can use fresh and dried leaves to make this fungicide.

This is also a very powerful fungicidal. Chop up 10 leaves of the Papaya. Grind. Dilute with 4 L of water, and either leave overnight, or apply right then.

So now, do not you think that it is much more worth it using than harmful chemical pesticides? Organic is best.

Remember to water the plants, where after you have applied any sort of pesticide. That is, so that any powerful effect of these pesticides is diluted.

Using Cow Manure Ash as a Pesticide

Now this may sound very messy to a Western farmer. But in the East, one has been using dried cow dung Ash as a pesticide for millenniums, to get rid of pests.

Cow dung cakes are burned to an ash. Normally, the dried cow dung, which was used as a producer of heat, while the food for the family was being cooked was collected out of the oven and then sprinkled all over the farm. This ash is still being used as a pesticide. Sprinkle some water on the affected plants. Then spray the ash powder by hand on those affected areas. This keeps the trees and the plants healthy.

These dried cow dung cakes are made by collecting cow dung, patting into patties and then dried on the side of the houses in rural India. This is still commonly used as a fuel by 60% of the people in the villages.

Nutrient Deficiency Symptoms in Plants

Any sort of nutrient deficiency in your plant is going to show up during June, July and August. That is when your plants are going well, and the changes in weather can show you how healthy your plants are or if they are suffering from any sort of nutrient deficiency.

Nitrogen deficiency – this is going to result in pale, yellow foliage and small leaves, thin and short shoots and hard and highly colored fruit.

Phosphorus deficiency – this is seen very seldom, but it is going to result in purple tinted foliage and restricted and thin shoots.

Potash deficiency – which can be rectified by adding bracken and seaweed to your plants and also comfrey water – is going to result in small, brittle, and sparse foliage. The margins of the leaf is going to be grayish – Brown. The shoots are going to be restricted and thin, and the fruit are going to be immature, small and dull.

Magnesium deficiency has brown scorching in the centers of the foliage. Shoots are spindly or absent in severe cases are elongated and thin in mild cases. Fruit is dull, immature and small.

Iron deficiency results in small fruit, bright yellow foliage, and reduced weight in harvest. Pears and apples are going to be pale green with a reddish flush on the fruit. This deficiency is mild if the outermost leaves of the tree are yellowish and the lower leaves are greener.

This is one of my favorite URLs, giving you extensive knowledge about nutrient deficiency and how you can get rid of it in your plants.
http://www.ghorganics.com/page32.html

Spraying

In order to counteract certain diseases and pests, it is necessary to spray your shrubs and plants from time to time, with a machine powerful enough to soak them all over.

When mixing the spray solution, follow the makers' directions carefully. Remember to cover your nose with a piece of cloth, or any other protected material, if you are using harsh and potentially poisonous pesticide sprays.

He would not need that covering over his nose, if he used natural pesticides.

Spray on a calm day and when the spray is not likely to be washed off by rain.

After spraying at the end of the season, pour away any unused solution down the drain. Do not keep it for the next spring. Wash the machine and the buckets thoroughly and oil all the removable parts of the spring equipment. Keep the hose in a dark place as strong sunlight is likely to destroy the rubber.

Garden Pests

Wasps, fruit flies, aphids, and other garden pests are definitely going to be a part of your garden. The moment your flowers and fruit start to make their appearance, apart from birds, and other harmful creatures, you are going to be inundated with garden pests.

This is an extremely helpful URL, where you are going to get information on how to control garden pests.

http://www.missouribotanicalgarden.org/gardens-gardening/your-garden/help-for-the-home-gardener/advice-tips-resources/pests-and-problems.aspx

Remember that harsh pesticides, especially when they have too much of chemical content in them is ultimately going to have a negative effect on your own health, especially when you are eating those apples and pears or preparing them for the market.

Pollination

Fruit trees are divided into two classes – self fertilizing or those trees which set from their own pollen and self-sterile – those which bear little or no fruit unless they receive pollen from some other variety of the same fruit blossoming at the same time.

Some days ago I read about a young student in a remote village in the mountains of India. She was extremely interested about the pollination process in apples, which come under the self-sterile category along with pears. She lives in an area which produces the most delicious apples exported all over the world. But the plant harvest depends a lot on pollination by insects, and that can be a chancy business for plants.

So she requested a nearby Apple Orchard farmer to allow her to do some experiments. She planted mustard plants under every visible apple tree. These yellow flowers attracted insects, and of course, they went to the apple blossoms too.

Naturally, that Apple Orchard owner has now a bumper crop of apples to sell in the market and to export abroad. He also is very glad of another unexpected bonus – mustard honey collected by his bees.

This young girl has been given awards from the state government for her imagination and her ability to work on that idea fruitfully, no pun intended and successfully.

So if your plants are sweet cherries, they are self-sterile. Plums can be self-sterile, partly self-sterile and partly self-fertile, depending on the variety. So started growing brightly flowering vegetables under your apple trees, and other fruit trees and get a green harvest along with a bumper fruit crop.

Fruit Plant Propagation

Fruit trees and bushes are propagated in various ways. Seedling fruits are invariably quite different from the parent varieties and so they cannot be relied upon. That is why you will need to use different methods of propagation including vegetative. This means the taking of cuttings, grafting and budding.

Budding and grafting are not easy. And for that reason, many gardeners by their plants from nursery men who specialize in producing first-class bushes and trees.

Logan berries, blackberries gooseberries red currants and black currants grow very well from cuttings. However, you need grafted or budded plants for cherries, pears, apples, damsons and plums. This is done by grafting them on certain wild types of the same family, which provide the root system known as rootstock.

You can know more about rootstock on this URL.

http://en.wikipedia.org/wiki/Rootstock

Grafting is normally carried out during the late winter months or in early spring, but budding is done during the summer months.

Harvesting your fruit

You need to take a lot of care during harvesting as it is not much use nurturing the fruit to the cropping stage, if it is going to be spoiled by incorrect harvesting. Experience is going to teach you not too pick to early or too late. Do not drop the fruit or bruise it.

I remember going through fruit farms in California, where harvesters were picking a bumper crop of fruit. Some of them did not mind polishing a ripe apple against their sleeves and taking a hefty bite. Then they dropped it down on the ground. Well, one cannot resist this, especially when your employer is not around, and you are harvesting grapes, strawberries and apples. It also shows that the harvester was enjoying his fruit picking activity in the sun and the air. But just imagine that fruit being crated in the box accidentally.

It is going to be almost as embarrassing and horrifying as the food tester on a product launching in *Biggles*, opening up a package of fast food, and found a chicken leg, out of which the idiotic partner had already taken a previous surreptitious bite.

So if you are picking fruit seriously, remember that the survival of the Orchard depends on the quality of the fruit and its packaging. Do not week in wet weather. Do not leave the fruit lying about in the sun. Do not put diseased fruit in with good fruit.

Appendix –

More useful URLs –

Fruit Trees – Planting and Care of Young Trees

HTTP://homeorchard.ucdavis.edu/8048.pdf

Conclusion

This is of course a beginner's guide on gardening, which is giving you the basics of choosing your plants, and growing them. The URLs are going to give you more information on the plants, which you can grow according to season and locality. Some plants start giving you a harvest in the first year itself, like strawberries. Other plants may take a while before you can get a bumper crop for them. But the effort is worthwhile, because whether you are gardening for pleasure or gardening for profit, you have greenery surrounding you.

So get out in the open air, enjoy the fruit of your labors – no pun intended – and Live Long and Prosper-The healthy way.

Author Bio

Dueep Jyot Singh is a Management and IT Professional who managed to gather Postgraduate qualifications in Management and English and Degrees in Science, French and Education while pursuing different enjoyable career options like being an hospital administrator, IT,SEO and HRD Database Manager/ trainer, movie scriptwriter, theatre artiste and public speaker, lecturer in French, Marketing and Advertising, ex-Editor of Hearts On Fire (now known as Solstice) Books Missouri USA, advice columnist and cartoonist, publisher and Aviation School trainer, ex- moderator on Medico.in, banker, student councilor ,travelogue writer … among other things! One fine morning, she decided that she had enough of killing herself by Degrees and went back to her first love -- writing. It's more enjoyable! She already has 48 published academic and 14 fiction- in- different- genre books under her belt.

When she is not designing websites or making Graphic design illustrations for clients , she is browsing through old bookshops hunting for treasures, of which she has an enviable collection – including R.L. Stevenson, O.Henry, Dornford Yates, Maurice Walsh, C.N.Williamson, Sapper, Bartimeus and the crown of her collection- Dickens "The Old Curiosity Shop," and so on… Just call her "Renaissance Woman") - collecting herbal remedies, acting like Universal Helping Hand/Agony Aunt, or escaping to her dear mountains for a bit of exploring, collecting herbs and plants and trekking.

Check out some of the other JD-Biz Publishing books

[Gardening Series on Amazon](#)

Health Learning Series

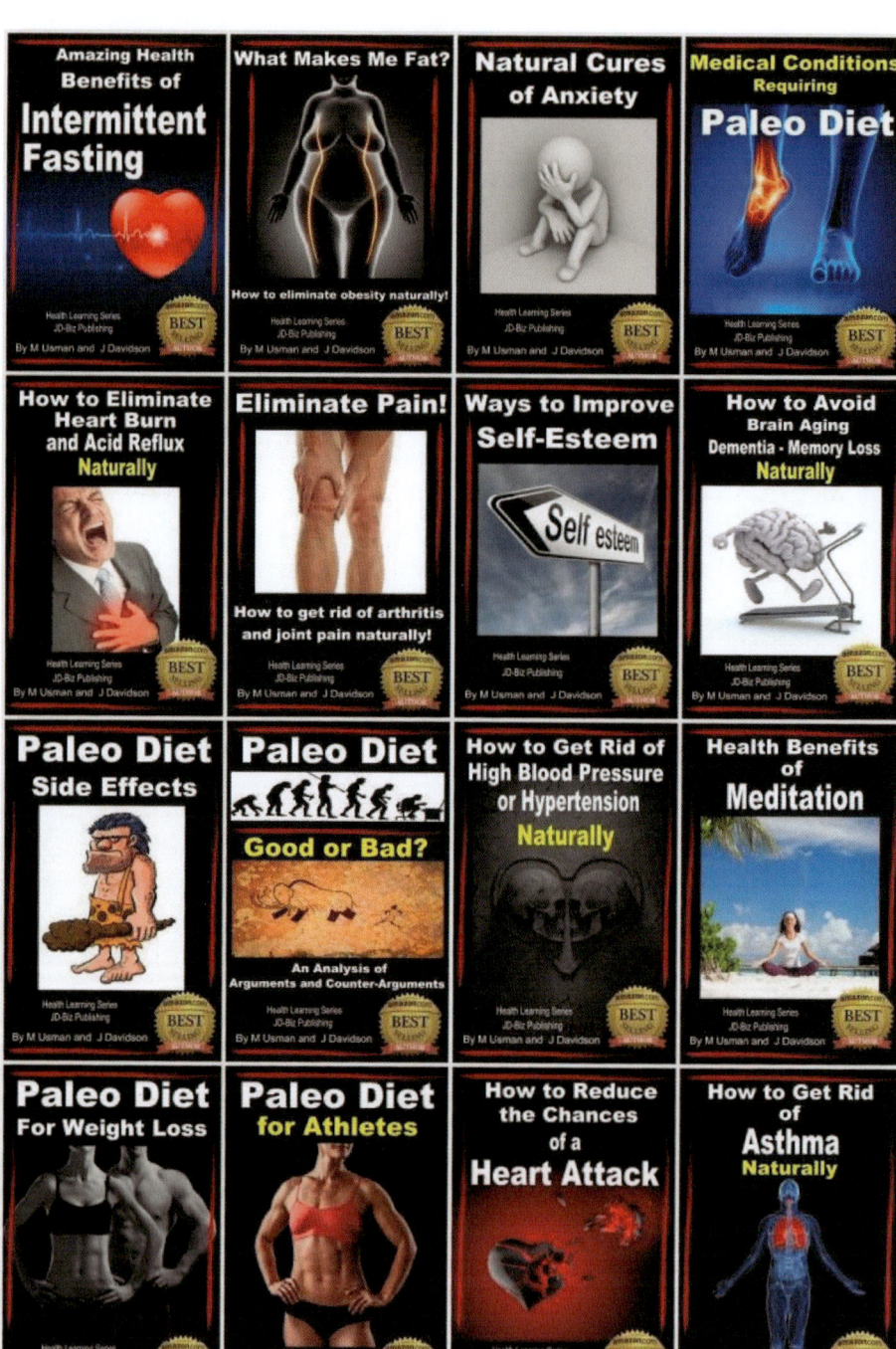

Amazing Animal Book Series

Learn To Draw Series

How to Build and Plan Books

Entrepreneur Book Series

Our books are available at

1. Amazon.com
2. Barnes and Noble
3. Itunes
4. Kobo
5. Smashwords
6. Google Play Books

Download Free Books!

http://MendonCottageBooks.com

Publisher

JD-Biz Corp

P O Box 374

Mendon, Utah 84325

http://www.jd-biz.com/